FUEL FOR THE MIND, BODY, AND SOUL

JOHN AND MICK TOSCANO

authorHOUSE

AuthorHouse™
1663 Liberty Drive
Bloomington, IN 47403
www.authorhouse.com
Phone: 833-262-8899

Published by AuthorHouse   09/16/2022

ISBN: 978-1-6655-7117-3 (sc)
ISBN: 978-1-6655-7116-6 (e)

Library of Congress Control Number: 2022917414

Print information available on the last page.

This book is printed on acid-free paper.

DEDICATION

Dedicated to our mother, Jackie, our true inspiration for beginning this journey of becoming published authors. Although she left us and her incomparable legacy as a mom on July 7, 2022, we were able to let her know that we accomplished our initial, shortest of term goal. It is, without a single doubt, clear and undeniably right that we properly honor her by continuing our newly realized legacy with publishing yearly editions of our thoughts of inspiration, motivation, and entertainment.

PREFACE

My brother and I have an incredible opportunity to motivate, inspire and entertain so many great people that may be in need of one or all of these goal-oriented emotions. Our genuine yet peculiar writings are designed around personal inspiration using acronyms and our own "thoughts for the day" in the most unique, yet fun approach with nothing more than the unavoidable impulse and compulsion for each reader to think, reflect, and laugh together. Each thought is yours to interpret and bring to life.

When people do not like dogs, there could be a problem. When a dog does not like a person, trust the dog.

ALWAYS

Anticipate tomorrow

Live, Laugh, Love and Learn

"Will it" to come to fruition

Asking for help makes you stronger

Your Family and Friends come first

See the good in everyone

Plan to work, work your plan.
Ideally: plan not to work.

Broke people owe a lot of money.
Homeless people are even.

BE

    Believe in you

    Express yourself

"I don't know where we're going…but we're making great time." …. Yogi Berra

It is always good when you finally
realize you may be good looking
but stay away from mirrors.

BEAUTY

Behold it

Everyone has it

Admire it

Ultimately it is in your heart

Take the time to see it in everything

Yours should be the first to be seen

Wake up and feel great. You have
the entire day to screw it up!

Beat anorexia...stay fat.

BEST

Believe that you are...

Every day tell yourself

Stay ahead of the game

Thank those who helped you along the way

Behave or just don't get caught.

Husband arrives home late.

CHARITY

Care genuinely for yourself

Have a giving heart

Appreciate the little things in life

Realize your ability to make an impact

Influence others to reach their potential

Take time for yourself

Your turn to make others feel great

Wife: "Drunk again?"

Husband: "Me too!" (Bad answer)

CHOICE

Create your own opportunities

Have a plan

Outline your strategies

Include your Team

Control the process

Eliminate any chance of failure

Sometimes you can find a home
through strangers in strange places.

Advice: Stay home!

COUNT

Cherish every minute

One day at a time

Use your time wisely

No time like the present

Time flies, maximize it

Whether it is 1 mile or 1,000 miles,
they both start with the first step.

"Leave the gun and take the cannoli's!" …. The God Father

ENJOY

Every day is another opportunity

Never say never

Jump up and down; it beats sitting

Over-celebrate you

Yell at the top of your lungs

Imagine what you did not do…and do it.

What do you admire more, the "painting" or the "painter?" Be the painter!

FAITH

Fear not

Acknowledge your values

Interpret what is right and true

Trust your heart

Hold strongly to your beliefs

Do you believe in miracles or yourself? Believe in both.

If you hit rock bottom, it makes
a wonderful place to start.

FAVOR

Forgive others; start with yourself

Aspire to perfection

Victory: believe you are a winner

Optimism over pessimism

Respect yourself first

There is no talent in quitting.

"Be yourself, everyone else is already taken." …. Oscar Wilde

FRIENDS

Forgive and forget

Realize how special they truly are

It is a privilege to have them

Every one of them is unique

Never be a bad one

Do not take them for granted

Savor the time with them

"I don't start counting my sit-ups until they start hurting." …. Muhammed Ali

When life is too dark to see,
it can only get brighter.

FUN

Feel it

Understand how to have it

Never forget the times when you had it

"Can Do" power is worthless
with "Can't Do" mentality.

Difficulty brings opportunity
to show your strength.

GIFT

Giving is better than receiving

It needs to be from the heart

Find time to give yours

Time with loved ones is the best gift of all

It takes a big person to face big problems.

'Even the mediocre people can identify a problem, but Superstars produce a solution.

GOOD

Greatness is in you

Opportunity is a door

Open it

Do it for others

Stronger is not always better. Being better makes you stronger.

Being loved is ordinary. Loving
someone is extraordinary.

GRACE

Giving is the ultimate form of gratification

Refine yourself towards dignity

Adorn those who extend it to you

Care genuinely about what you do and say

Embrace your ability to share yours

You never realize you are alone until you are.

Family and Friends mean so much.
Make sure they feel the same for you.

GREAT

Generate momentum to be….

Realize you are….

Each day is…

Attribute yours to those who shared theirs

Tell others they are….

Do not let schooling get in the
way of your education.

Instead of fighting with each other, joust. The horse ride is well worth it.

HONOR

Have it

Own it

Need it

Offer it

Recognize it

There is nothing worse than a male bartender at Happy Hour.

Take off your shoes when you enter someone's home but keep your socks on.

HOPE

Have realistic goals

Open you mind to all options

Possibilities are endless

Exceed your expectations

Music changed the world...sing your song!

Breaking one egg in a carton can
be disappointing. Just remember
you have eleven more.

DO IT

Demand something positive of yourself daily

Overcome obstacles

Initiate your innovations

Teach what you learned

If you think your performance was poor, you
are one act away from a standing ovation.

People leave jobs because of bad managers. Managers leave jobs because of bad leaders. Leaders leave jobs because of bad culture. The unemployed don't care.

LEARN

Listen

Every day is another opportunity

Acquire as much knowledge as possible

Respect those who taught you

Never stop your pursuit

There is a terrible thing that happens if you do not advertise...NOTHING. Advertise you!

"Timid salesmen have skinny
kids." …. Zig Ziglar

LEAST

Love yourself

Every day, call someone (no email, no text)

Accept the fact that you are human

See the true you every day

"Take Five"...for yourself everyday

"Whether you think you can, or you think
you can't – you're right," …. Henry Ford

What you lost is not as important
as what you can still find.

LIFE

Live it to the fullest

Impact everyone you touch

Find something memorable everyday

Expect peaks and valleys; enjoy the ride

The more successful you become,
the more critics you will encounter.

Go where you are celebrated, not
where you are just tolerated.

LISTEN

Learn from your mistakes

Initiate conversation

Shhhh…. silence is golden

Talk less

Engage in controversy

Naysayers have value too

When it comes to offering your opinion
or critique, take the high road…
there is much less traffic up there.

There is more honor in aiming your goals too high and missing than aiming your goals too low and hitting.

LIVE

Leave your worries behind

Embrace in every moment of your life

Visualize all aspects of your life; conquer your bucket list

End each day completely satisfied

Be a half hour early, never a minute late.

Responsibility comes in the most responsible
form when people try to catch up to
you, even when you are in a slump.

LOVE

Let it flow

Open your heart

Vow to share yours

Embrace it

What other people think of YOU
is none of YOUR business.

Look not for excuses, look for innovation.

ME

    Mold yourself into the absolute best YOU

    Enjoy your progress

Do not wait for a special occasion…
every day is special.

The probability of you stumbling
upon success...is ZERO!

MIND

Making up yours can be tough; tackle the
challenges

Incredible ones think alike

Never to be wasted

Dream big

Courtesy flush...Please!

Please return your stewardess to
her normal, upright position.

MONEY

Make it

Offer it

Never stop working for it

Enjoy it

You deserve it

Cold is a temperature; warmth is a feeling.

You can always dig to put in a tree
but use your hands to plant it.

NEVER

Never leave room for negativity

Eliminate "never", replace with "forever"

Visionaries don't stop dreaming

Even in times of doubt, "never" lose hope

Respect today like tomorrow may never come

Birds fly…that's what they do. Soar.

You can always buy soup in
a can. Make your own.

ONE

Opinion; share yours

Never back down from your gut or your heart

Endure your criticism

Water can boil. Don't let it scald you.

It's beautiful to see flowers
grow. Be the flower.

PLAY

Personality; make your magnetic

Lots of laughs

Actions speak louder than words

You already won

Vines make grapes. Grapes
make wine. Be the vine.

Comedy makes you laugh. It's the comedian that makes you smile.

PULL

Power through the opposition

Use your strengths

Leave the past behind

Lift your spirits; tug on your dreams

The spectrum can be combined to make all colors. But rainbows provide them.

Dogs can poop in your home ANYWHERE, but they bring joy to your home EVERYWHERE.

PUSH

Propel yourself

Utilize your resources

Slay your dragons

Have a relentless drive towards success

Thoughts lead to novels. Edits make them better. Edit your novel!

Sometimes you hit rapids in your canoe with only one paddle. Always do whatever it takes to stay afloat.

RACE

Realize your potential

Attack the improbable

Chase the impossible

Enjoy crossing the finish line

Santa brings gifts every year.
Share your gifts every day.

Words are "good." Lyrics make "good"
- "better." Songs make "better" –
"great." But silence is still "golden!"

REACT

Run; don't walk

Elevate interest

Acquire knowledge

Create demand

Treasure the journey

When you meet someone, you like, take
the time to actually "meet" them.

Buds turn into flowers. Enjoy the bloom.

REST

    Relax and enjoy life

    Every day, kiss yourself

    Still your mind

    Take time to smell the roses

Admire your elders, as you will be one day.

Reading educates…watching
the movie saves the time.

SEE

Step forward, don't look back

Eyes on tomorrow

Envision your potential

Cooking is fun. Eating is better. Clean
up sucks! (I love my dishwasher)

Savor the moments that make
you the maddest. Learn!

STOP

Sit and think

Take a mental break

Opt out of nonsense; opt in for common sense

Pull over; enjoy the view

Shower at least three times a week!

Wake up every morning. Take advantage of that opportunity.

SELF

Stand tall

Exception; be one

Luminate your aura

Feel right about you

Be the greatest you can be. Don't waste this opportunity on trying to be great like somebody else.

Say what you mean. Mean what
you say. And stand by it.

SELL

Showcase your value

Expose your talents

Lead by example

Luck; create your own

Settling for mediocrity will only lead to that.

It is much more rewarding to have a life of significance than a life of success.

SPIRIT

Spend your time wisely

Please yourself to please others

Innovate and motivate

Reach high

I can, I will

Test yourself by taking chances

Expectations are obsolete until you commit.

Thinking creates possibilities. Possibilities make you think. Think everything is possible.

STAR

Shoot for one

Thank your lucky one

Act like one

Realize you are one

You don't have to be great to be good, but you do have to be good to be great.

Construct your surroundings
to build your character.

THRIVE

Tenacity is a must

Have Courage

Reassure yourself

Ignite a fire within yourself

Vision and direction lead to completion

Encourage others to....

Hold onto your dreams, especially
when you wake up.

Ideas are just ideas. Dreams are just dreams. When you put those two together, you can bring them to life.

TIME

Take advantage of it

It's precious

Make it count

Each day; it's a gift

The smallest pieces of a chocolate chip cookie are the chips. What would it be without them?

Do you ever feel like you are dime in a bucket of nickels? You are half the size but worth twice as much.

TRUE

Total honesty

Righteousness

Understand that you can't lie to you

Ethics; be unquestionable

Everybody loves corned beef on St. Patty's Day, but what would it be without the cabbage?

When you're alone, enjoy your time.

VISION

Visit life

Include you in yours

See your potential

Illuminate your path

Open eyes, open mind, open doors

Nothing is impossible

There is no one to argue with in the mirror.

No one can tell you, "You
have to" except you.

WIN

Work smarter, not harder

I can and I will

Never settle if your best can be better

Going through a maze can be confining
and confusing…jump "a-hedge."

Mowing the lawn seems so burdensome,
but you'll just love the results?

WISDOM

We all have it

Invite others to share theirs

Seek it from your elders

Do whatever it takes to gain it

Offer to share it

Master the art of finding it

Mail letters. The receivers will
appreciate the stamp.

Saying "yes" is easy but saying "no" might be more rewarding.

WORK

Wealth and wisdom are results of it

One's dignity peaks from it

Recognize and reward other people's

Know that yours can help so many

If people bore you, spend five minutes in the mirror.

When you are searching for something,
be prepared for what you might find.

NOW

No time like the present

On time is late, early is on time

Waiting is not an option

Funny is laughable. Comedy is
thought generating. Combine them
and it becomes an occupation.

Better to be with someone who doesn't make you laugh than someone that makes you cry.

YOU

Yearn for perfection

Own your individuality

Utilize your gifts

Sometimes the unexpected is better than the expected.

Actors are performers. Performs
are actors. Be the Director.

CHANGE

Convert yourself to a better place

Hang up the old school thinking

Adjust to whatever makes you better and
different

Nothing should hold you back

Give everything new your best shot

Exchange ideas with the experts

Your intentions are who you want
to be; intend to be YOU.

Getting from here to there takes
a drive. Take a walk instead.

CLARITY

Clear your mind COMPLETELY

Logic needs to be your new focus

Articulate your vision and direction

Rationality takes priority over insanity

Intellect is your strength

Think…

Your heart works in tandem with your wisdom

Bloodlines stand the test of time.
Enjoy your next picnic.

Never get into an argument with an idiot, as
they will beat you down with experience.

CLUTTER

Confusion is the reason for it

Lack of ability is just an excuse

Untidiness is a habit you can break

Test yourself daily with organization

Tranquility is the start of your resolution

Renew, Refurbish, and Regulate to Restore
Peace in your life

Be careful who you care for.

Your eyes can always see beauty...
no need to where glasses.

DISCIPLINE

Decide on a goal

Initiate a strategy

Self-control is something only you can monitor

Charge your mind, body, and soul with a daily inspiration

Inspiration to continue can be found in mysterious places and people

Promise yourself that today is going to be successful

Learn what limitless means to you

Insist on achieving your daily goal

Normal for you should be remarkable to the rest

Empower yourself as if you were your own employee

All goals are attainable. Score!

Winning a marathon is great, but finishing is just as rewarding.

DISCOVER

Dream the impossible

Innovation will always override excuses

See something no one else can see

Convince yourself that the truth is your conclusion

Overcome every obstacle

Value the oppositions

Encounter what others could never see

Realize that your process and program are right

People don't always care when you know, but they always know when you care.

Would you hire you?

EMOTIONAL

Enthusiasm

Master the art of motivating people

Over celebrate every opportunity

Thrill the people you touch

Impressions...leave the positive ones

Outpouring but never outspoken

Noble and Notable.... make it memorable

Affectionate

Lovable, but more importantly, loving

If you are going to make a
mistake, be unique.

If what you are seeing raises
doubts, change the channel.

INSPIRE

It's not an individual "sport"

Nobody should be without it, especially if it is
up to you

Stimulate your mind, your body, and your soul
first

Persuasion is only useful when it is mutually and
equally beneficial

Initiate a conversation…not a presentation

Revive your enthusiasm first

Encourage those who may never had
experienced this

If you find a fly in your
chardonnay, drink around it.

When you get off "the throne,"
don't forget your crown.

INTENTION

Intelligence can bring about independent

Notions can bring about confidence

Tenacity can bring about intensity

Enthusiasm can bring about emphasis

Nothing should break your focus

Train your mind to see a target in the most darkest of times

Imagine your achieving your goal

One goal at time while you take one day at a time

Nothing will be more noticeable to you, while nothing will be more noticeable to others

Have ever woke up in the morning and said to yourself, "I may or may not owe some people some handwritten apologies?"

Find your spy that will keep your secrets safe.

LEGACY

Leave yours

Expectations of you from others can only be exceeded by you

Grant someone very dear to you the gift to carry one together

Attribute yours to those who cared enough about you be sure you have one

Capability is different from responsibility...you need both

Yours is only yours until you share it.... it's up to you

Enjoy people who may be just half great.

You may be invisible at times, but
you are always invaluable.

PHYSICAL

Powerful

Healthy

Youthful

Significant

Influential

Congenial

Available

Living, Laughing, Loving

Relationships can encounter turbulence
at sea; be a great captain.

Living life is a privilege, loving life is a virtue.

POWER

Potency of your words to be shared with others

Overbearing will never make you influential

Work to your full capacity...with your Team

Exercise your most important muscle...your brain

Reign over your mind, body, and soul only...you have the ability to strengthen others

Sometimes OK is great.

Look in the mirror and smile every day.

PURPOSE

Principles are yours to keep

Use your rational thinking...simple common sense

Resolutions come naturally with this sense

Point your mind, body, and soul directly towards the shortest distance to your goal

Object strenuously when you find yourself without one

Single-mindedness is a necessity to avoid single madness

Excuses end now...replace with your renewed sense of innovation

Be ecstatic with YOU.

Be YOU every day.

SIMPLE

Straightforward

Ingenious

Modest

Principles

Limitless

Effortless

Be your own elevator and press
the top floor button every day.

People always forgive you. Don't
be so quick to forgive yourself.

SPIRITUAL

Sacred to you and only you

Psychic...not psychotic

Inspiration comes from our mind, body, and soul

Revery; find this place where everyone is
respected

Ideals have to be realistic and believable

True to life is more interesting than fiction

Unfaithful is what will be brought to those who
are no longer reliable

Authenticity is good when it benefits more than
just you

Loyalty to your beliefs will bring the ultimate
feeling of Love

Life can be fragile...stay away from glass.

Honesty depends on you.

PASSION

Pull for something important to come true for
someone else

Appetite for this should be unwavering

Starving for this will result in desperate measures

Striving for this will result in true fulfillment

Infatuation works so much better in numbers
than all alone

Obsession is not a healthy form of it

Notoriety comes only to those who shares theirs

It's easy to see things with our
eyes closed. Keep them open.

Golfing alone is easy...get in
the cart with someone.

CAPTIVATE

Charming

Attracting

Pleasuring

Transfixing

Intriguing

Validating

Appealing

Tempting

Enthralling

Jalapeños are hot...be the Ghost Pepper.

Yelling is loud…silence is louder.

THINK

Try, try, try again

Hold on to your first thought

Imagine the benefits of completion

No stone unturned throughout the process

Know more what not to do than what you imagine you can do

Microwaves cook fast, ovens cook slow…just grill!

Doctor visits can be scary, Dentist visits can give anxiety, just get a mani-pedi instead!

SEEK

Strive for the answer

Enquire about who, what, where, when and why

Escape from your past thinking

Keep the faith that you will always find your way out of the woods

You can shower or take a bath and think.

Orchestras are made up of many
pieces, make yours heard.

SHARPEN

Seek out the sharpest of knives to whittle away
the bark

Home in on your goal

Ask yourself, "What you do I want for the
answer?"

Relax and expand your mind to think clearly

Put all your thoughts in your mind down on paper

Expect bumps in the road, and explain them
away

Nothing is perfect, but today you will be as sharp
as you've ever been

Play in the playground that you create.

Sandcastles have boundless
possibilities...build yours.

INSIGHT

Images turn into ideas

Notice your surroundings and challenges

Sagacity will come to you just as wisdom came
to others

Ideas turn into reality

Gain knowledge with every failure

High-powered thinking is a result from the
knowledge from failures

Test your perception daily with your astuteness
and wisdom

Houses are what you build...homes
are where memories begin.

Air is free...take time to enjoy
it...the price is right.

ADVANTAGE

Always know you have one

Defeat belongs to someone else

Validate your thoughts with proof

Advance your thinking

No speed limit in the pursuit of excellence

Take the leap of faith before anybody else

Acquire the knowledge and strength before you
test yourself

Gain the lead at every opportunity

Enjoy the journey of winning

Driving is so much fun based
on your destination.

Rain is common, Thunder is loud, Lightning is scary...look forward to the rainbow.

SECURE

Safety is found with those you trust

Ensure you provide it for those you love

Confidence in yourself is the best place to start

Use your heart and mind to strengthen your confidence

Reliability is a great quality others need to see in you to feel it

Everyone needs it, so bring it to those who don't have it

Leaves on trees may fall...
they always come back.

Knowing who you are cannot get any better.

SMART

Sharpen your mind, not just your pencil

Motivation creates inspiration

Apply yourself learning lessons in life

Reinvent yourself with brainpower and imagination

Train your brain to focus

Patios and decks are great…it's what you put on them defines you.

Making clay plates, pots, and mugs
is an art. Never turn off your kiln.

MIRROR

Model yourself to be admirable

Impressions are made first whether or not they
are good or bad

Reflections are what you see in one and what
others see in you without one

Represent yourself with modesty, honesty, and
your unique personality

Only you can change the person you see in it

Reveal all that you see while looking in one, then
remove what you don't like

Light bulbs bring light...what surrounds
them makes them bright.

Carpet needs to be vacuumed; hardwood needs to be mopped...don't we all?

GENIUS

Give the gift of wisdom to those who ask you for it

Even the experts continue their education

No one stumbles upon it; it is an acquired characteristic

Ingenuity is rare, but not in you

Understanding how to share it is more important than what you share

Showcase your talents with other for benefitting, not bragging

Blankets make you warm...who you share them with makes them warmer.

Walking downstairs is easy...walking up gives you something to look forward to.

LIMIT

Leave your constraints behind

Imagine what you can accomplish without them

Maximize your potential with motivation

Innovation comes to those who eliminate boundaries

Test the untested to make impossible the possible

Liking is temporary...Loving is forever.

Friends may come and go...
true ones stay forever.

LEAD

Lend a hand to those behind you

Encourage everyone to be their best by your examples

Allow mistakes, then guide to the resolution

Direction and Vision is an incredible responsibility, so take it

Shake someone's hand, just
remember who shook yours.

Yawning is contagious, better
yet...so is smiling.

TOGETHER

Time spent with loved ones is priceless

Opportunities to spend that time should never be rare

Gratification comes in many forms, spending time with loved ones is the greatest

Embrace each experience, life is too short

Tomorrow offers no guarantee, so spend time today

Have this as a habit, not an event

End each day having spent the time as if it were your last

Remember the best times spent

Indoors...limited; outdoors..." UN..."

Clouds may cover the sun but take
the time to enjoy the shade.

READY

Rely on yourself

Envision the finish line

Anticipate all the challenges; have all the
answers

Discipline comes from no one else but you

Your ability to prepare your mind, body separates
you from the rest

Love your in-laws, especially when
they're away on vacation.

Patience is mentally self-driven… "think" about it.

WILLING

Wanting and wishing are only dreams

Inspiration moves you to participation

Lead with passion

Love the cause

Initiate the plan

Now is your time, nothing can stop you now

Give it all you got

Would you rather be a whale in an ocean or a piranha in a goldfish tank?

When it comes to pudding,
don't be the tapioca .

ABLE

Amazing things happen when you apply yourself outside your comfort zone

Be the exception, not the statistic

Leave memorable experiences with your extraordinary accomplishments

Exceed your expectations and aim higher with every challenge

Smart people may come up with some answers, geniuses listen to every question.

Statistics can make you a great mathematician, logic can make you a great psychologist, science can make you a great physicist, dreamers are not categorized.

NO

Not an option

Only YOU can make that call

Bubbles pop...keep blowing.

Enjoy a bath, enjoy a jacuzzi, enjoy
a sauna, shower to be clean.

WORK

Will it in you; and be the best at it

Orchestrate it

Reward yourself

Know you did it

Beer and wine loosen you up, liquor makes
you fun, shots lead you to stupidity.

Personalities are as unique as
looks…appreciate both.

DREAM

Desire to be who you want to be

Realize that they can come true

Aim to attain them

Make them happen

Flowers make everyone happy…
buy some for yourself.

Convey your message through your heart and soul...shouldn't take long.

COACH

Council

Overcome losses

Address the roster

Count on your players

Herald and stand by your decisions

Don't call on friend because you need one, call because you want to make one.

Don't ever stop thinking.

FLY

Fear no heights

Leap upward

Yank hard on the ties that bind you

The first step in educating
yourself is enrolling.

TV dinners are the worst invention ever, make dinner and sit down together.

SOLID

Stay strong

Ostracize negativity

Land on your feet

Institute the strength in you

Drive the rock

Turn the TV off.

Find ways to enhance your
articulation, make them think.

GOLD

Great is better than good

Organize your bars

Loyalty awakes your Royalty

Dig deep

If you are not in the conversation,
it might be about you.

Sunshine in comfortable…enjoy the rain.

SHAME

    Stay away from it

    Have class

    Assure you never fear it

    Mistakes are OK

    Exemplify YOU

Clouds may block the sun, but
they always move along.

You might have to rent a crane to erect your building, if that doesn't work, buy one.

ACCEPT

Any critiques

Create your market

Concede your losses

Excuses are not an option

Perfection

Total gratification

The toughest part about working out is the drive to the gym.

Spare change may not mean a
lot until you fill a bucket.

SOUL

Savor YOU

Only YOU know where yours stands

Use YOU to make others better

Leave no stone unturned until you turn your own

How many "nos" does it take to
get a "yes" …doesn't matter.

Marriage is wonderful…try to limit them.

EGO

Either you have it, or you will never get it

Greatness in you in eternal

Obtain yours

Listen to your heartbeat…it has a lot to say.

If you struggle at putting,
work on your chipping.

RAGE

Rant for what you believe

Attack

Go with it maturely

Endeavour confidently

Water and sun make things bloom, be both.

The best athletes are the fastest, strongest, and most agile...but look at Tom Brady

HIGH

Hold your head up

Involve yourself with people that take you

Grab your string and control your kite

Herald no boundaries

Keep up with the news, everyone needs a good laugh.

When it comes to life, have a mission.
"A.B.C." …" Always Be Creating".

ROLL

Reacting is sometimes better than jumping the gun

Overcome objections

Leave worries

Love YOURSELF…YOU are the one!

Saying sorry is proper, feeling sorry is human.

If challenges ever cease, you will never grow.

FUEL

Figure out the gas that drives

Use it

Engage your mental tank with it

Love the smell

Power may be great, money may be
powerful, but love is priceless

Don't be afraid to put cinnamon
on your toast.

PAY FOR IT

Prepare for controversy

Address it

Yearning for more only makes you better

Fear not in the process

Relish the expense

I can make it happen

Trials and tribulations make the cost so much
easier to understand

There are tests of times, and times you
are tested, stand the tests of time

If you want to impress people,
impress yourself.

BIG RIGS

Be one

Intent to use all 18 wheels

Grip the road

Ride hard

Idle sometimes

Going slow and steady can get you their faster

Stay in your lane

Popsicles, Fudgesicles, and Ice Cream
Sandwiches…go "Klondike". ™

Moon moves tides, tides move
sand…walk in both.

REV

Rejuvenate YOU every day

Energize others

Vitalize your talent

Bars and Restaurants are fun, parties
are great, galas are unbelievable…
no place like home.

You can wake up mad, sad, or
glad...it's your choice.

TIRE

Treads make them

Ingenuity creates them

Rubber "souls" bind them

Enthusiasm perfects them

See what others can't see, then
lend them your eyes.

Try not to come second in a stupid contest.

HORN

Heed

Observe

Respect

Never ignore

If you are looking to hire someone who is dedicated, honest and hard-working, hire me and I'll help you look.

If you ever feel down and out,
go to a laundromat.

EXPECT

Each ride is another opportunity to make memories

X-tra time to prepare

Plan for potholes along the road

Expedite your route

Create new ones on ever trip

Take the fork in the road

When your employee tells you that they just don't feel like working today, let them know that you have never said that you don't feel like paying them today.

The amount of time you spend on problematic people takes away from the time you can spend with the Super Stars.

JET

>   **J**ourney

>   **E**xcel

>   **T**urbo

>   Talk to people, don't text them.

There is a huge difference between
being a "speaker" and a "teacher".

SPEED

Show your top….

Pedal to the "metal"

Expect more

Exceed most

Deliver

Perfect your skill in finding someone
in the act of excellence.

Greatness should be a habit...not an event.

SPRINT

    See the finish line

    Pass the tape first

    Race hard

    Initiate the chase

    Never walk alone

    Track your time

Be tough, but more importantly, be fair.

Positively start each day positive.

BURN

Be the one to start the fire

Usher in the kindling

Reignite to stay hot

Never lose your spark

Make sure the people in your circle of trust believe that you are a valuable resource.

Electricity makes light, firewood
makes fire, trees make paper...
make something on your own.

QUICK

Qualify your time

Use it wisely

Ignite your fire

Conquer your dreams

Kill it

Shower every day, or at least make
an attempt to run the water.

Brush your teeth…no matter
how many you have.

STOP

See the red

Tread lightly

Opt to be colorblind

Pause: prepare to go

Candles don't last forever, so enjoy
the flame…and keep it burning.

Every occupation serves a purpose...take time to say, "Thank you for your service."

LEFT LANE

Leave it when you can

Ease into the middle

Fast isn't always quicker

Try steady

Love all three lanes

Any lane will get you there

No need to miss the view

Enjoy your passenger(s)...always

Hitting a pitch in baseball is difficult...keep swinging.

HOME

Have one

Only YOU know how much it means

Make it a forever place

Enjoy the comfort of it

TOLLS

Take the time to pay them

Overcome their costs

Leave them behind

Look forward to the next one...you are closing in on your destination

Save your change

OPEN ROADS

Opportunities

Pave yours

Endure them

Negotiate

Read the signs

Open your eyes

Address your options

Deliver

Stay your path

TIME

Treasure it

It's not guaranteed

Measure it by what you do

Embellish your trek

POWER

Push

Own

Work

Exhibit

Reach

PATH

Pick the right one

Attack it with a purpose

Take your own

Have the patience for whatever road you choose

STEER

Strong drivers learn from their passion

The best runners know where to take them

Encourage your partners

Exemplify your leadership

Respect all in your route

PUMP

Press hard

Use some muscle

Make sure you fill up every day

Put some in your reserve tank

PRICE

Put into perspective

Realize you get what you pay for

Initiate your worth

Convey it

Expect it

SEMIS

Stay bigger

Enjoy your grandeur

Make sure yours is clean and strong

Idolize who you hook up with

See you there soon

MERGE

Make sure the coast is clear

Enjoy the union

Remember those who got you where you are

Go forward

Enter the right lane

YIELD

Youth starts with precautions

Ideas help you grow

Education makes you smarter

Life is the best lesson from which you can learn

Driving can make you brilliant…avoid the yellow lights

NO CROSSING

Never overstep

Obey your heart

Consider your perceptions

Life is the best lesson you can learn

Driving can make you brilliant…there's no yellow lights

Recognize it

Observe your signs

Stop and think

Sometimes step aside

Intersections may slow you down but won't stop you

No need to redirect

Go, Go, Go

ADMIRE

Appreciate the greatness with what you are surrounded

Distinguish its uniqueness

Marvel at its value

Imitate what you love

Respect both the art and the artist

Endorse whole heartedly

ADORE

Advocate your perception

Defend your appreciation

Offer your feelings

Reverence has no bias

Evolve to find so many more

APPRECIATE

Attach your heart to things that matter

Pay attention

Praise only takes a second

Revere those who came before you

Engage with those who move you

Create your circle of trust

Initiate a time to get together

Acknowledge your family first

Tell them

Evaluate yourself

AMUSE

Act a fool once in a while

Make a joke where everyone can laugh

Use your mistakes as a punchline

Smiling paints your picture

End each day with those memories

ANGER

Avoid the temptation

Never go to bed with it

Get rid of the minutia

Expedite a resolution

Rise above

ANXIETY

Ask what will turn you around

Nervousness is only nerves

X-out the negative

Identify the positive

Elevate your logic

Take time to breath

YOU will overcome

AWE

Amaze YOU first

Wonderment is within YOU

"Extra" is the first word in "extraordinary"

AWKWARD

Accept that we all are

Work your way out

Know how talented you are

Weird? No...UNIQUE

Ask yourself what is different

Rare is not risky, it's rewarding

Design your life in your own way

BORED

Be creative

"Over and Over" needs to be over!

Routine needs to be broken!

Enhance your imagination

Discover your innovativeness; invent something today

CALM

Compose your body

Appease your mind

Listen to your heart

Magnify your soul

CONFUSED

Clear your mind

Open your heart

Note the issue

Forget the past

Use your gut

State your goal

Execute your plan

Delight in your success

CRAVE

Care

Revere

Admire

Value

Examine

DISGUST

Don't dwell

Identify options

Stop the madness

Garbage In, Garbage Out

Unclutter your emotions

Switch direction

Turn the page

PAIN

Push through the hard spots

Aches are sign of hard work

It takes dedication and commitment to work toward results

Negate it because you are a winner!

ENTRANCED

Enamored

Noticed

Tuned

Riveted

Absorbed

Nominated

Charmed

Engrossed

Delighted

PAST

Pay attention to yours and others'...there is much to learn

Aches are pains have been suffered by so many...take advantage of what they learned

See your future based on your successes you've already achieved

Take your time to make great decisions never to repeat the past

PRESENT

Push yourself into a new way of spending today

Remove the negativity of yesterday, and bring on the positivity of right now

Every moment that is presented to you is another opportunity to change

Start each day by reading your affirmations and goals

Each sunrise is a gift...a present for only you to open

Now is the time, as procrastination is not an option

Tomorrow may be too late...get this party started

FUTURE

Forgive, forget, and forge ahead

Understand the value of the gift of another second, minute, hour, and day

Talk it through, buy yourself, and believe what was thought to be impossible is possible

Utilize all your resources, as there is no talent in quitting

Reveal to yourself what is most important for tomorrow, as yesterday cannot be changed

Events in the past do not define you…it's what you do tomorrow that dignifies who you are and what you represent

HEART

Have one

Enjoy others'

Acknowledge what yours can do for others

Realize the potential in yours

Test yours without conditions

DANCE

Do it; good, bad, or ugly

Act like you have the best

Never stop
Create your own
Enjoy the music

END

Exists only in Fairytales; you're not in one

No such thing if you don't include one in your story

Done with one chapter, begin the next; keep writing your story

Printed in the United States
by Baker & Taylor Publisher Services